THINK LIKE A
LAWYER

Eyitayo Ogunyemi

Copyright © 2020

All rights reserved.
No part of this book may be reproduced or
transmitted in any form or by any means, electronic or mechanical,
including photocopying, recording, or by any information
storage and retrieval system,
without written permission from the author.

Published by:
Heart2World Publishing
info@heart2worldpublishing.org

For information on distributions, translations, or bulk sales,
please contact
Eyitayo Ogunyemi

CONTENT

Let's Break Some Walls!	6
Introduction	8
Much Ado About Making Deals	11
Offer	14
Can An Offer Be Made To Unascertained Persons?	23
Cross Offer	27
Counter Offer	31
Termination of Offer	36
Acceptance	41
Consideration	49
Intentions in Relationships	54
Situations of Invalid Contract Entry	58

Misrepresentation	61
Mistake	67
Duress	73
Undue Influence	78
Illegality	80
Basic Points To Consider Before The Contract	84
Contract Defaults and How to Handle them	96
Frustration of Contract	108
Letting Go and Moving on from Relationships	117
Write It	124

LET'S BREAK SOME WALLS

In secondary school, I was probably the worst mathematics student because I gave up on attempting mathematical tasks before even trying. Years after, I came to a realisation that my challenge was not that I was never going to understand mathematics, but that my mind was zeroed on never trying to understand it.

In the same way, there are many non-lawyers who would probably not like to have anything to do with LAW. Not because they can never understand it, but because they already have a mindset that "it is not their thing" and "the language of law is convoluted."

The thought of calculating my client's fees and ensuring the right fees usually made my aversion to mathematics disappear, while I focus on the basics of getting the job done.

This is similar to law; the moment you see the strategic advantage that your knowledge of basic legal principles gives you on the negotiation table, then it becomes easier to apply yourself to the discipline.

This book offers you insights on principles of law for business transactions. It helps you improve your general knowledge of the law such that you know how to make valid deals, make more money, build more networks, and be a strategic deal maker.

The first thing you must give up is that limitation that says you cannot understand law; you can understand anything you commit to understanding.

I do not promise that you will become a lawyer after reading this book, but you will become smarter at making deals. It's time to acquire a better legal awareness for your deals and be a strategic decision maker who leverages the understanding of law to structure deals, make better decisions, and better businesses.

Introduction

The legal profession uses words as its instrument. Many professional negotiators and deal brokers have a background in law as a discipline. This is not surprising because lawyers are trained to canvass, mediate, advocate and negotiate. The best of lawyers are therefore often times masters of words, not because syntax is part of their discipline, but because they have an understanding of words within the context of law.

To a grammarian, "best endeavour" may mean the same thing as "reasonable endeavour", but not to a lawyer! The intention might be to ensure that effort is made to get results, but the business-minded lawyer understands that "best endeavour" is subjective while "reasonable endeavour" is objective.

You therefore need to think like a lawyer to dissect transactions and straighten contractual situations. The skills include interpersonal skills and the knowledge of the laws relating to interpersonal relationships. These skills help you identify the areas of which you can take advantage in deals and the pitfalls to avoid.

You might have attended a session on contract principles or read a book on law before coming across this one. None would have done the work of simplifying the subject as much as this book sets out to do. If the subject of law is not one of those things you like, this book mixes humour and practicality with learning.

This book is highly recommended for entrepreneurs, deal makers, professional negotiators and business executives. Law students trying to establish a foundation for making an excellent grade in the course will also find it handy.

This book explains the basics of the law of contractual relationship in a plain way; it establishes first that contracts are not only found in the complex transactions of life, but also in the most elementary dealings too. With that in mind, it describes the workings of the key elements of contract; OFFER, ACCEPTANCE and CONSIDERATION through a social relationship. Lessons are pointed out through the social relationship as readers are walked through other areas of law that they need to master.

Please note that the characters in this book are fictitious and are not intended to refer to any person.

Similarly, the social relationship demonstrated between Joe and Eve may not qualify as an enforceable contract in legal parlance, it only serves to demonstrate how contract works from the most elementary perspective.

MUCH ADO ABOUT MAKING DEALS

Call it a deal or a contract, there are peculiar things common to both. A contract is an AGREEMENT and it takes at least two people to create one. The basis of CONTRACT is that we are social beings whose behaviour is capable of affecting others.

The book ROBINSON CRUSOE by Daniel Defoe is handy in explaining this. The character referred to as Robinson Crusoe found himself on an island as a result of a shipwreck.

Upon combing the island, he found that he was the only one there, he therefore had little or no rules to set for himself as he would not have to enforce against himself, a breach of his own self-made rules.

However, one eventful day, he met another person on his island whom he named "Man Friday". With Man Friday in the picture, there was a need to set rules and orders and in essence make contract.

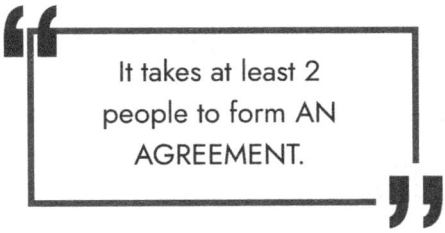

> It takes at least 2 people to form AN AGREEMENT.

The lesson from Robinson Crusoe is that SOCIAL RELATIONSHIPS lead to contracts. If you are in a world of your own and not dealing with anybody, you probably do not need to bind yourself to contracts. Even some laws that are government-created, agreement to resume at work at a specific time, etc. are examples of contract. So, you find that contract is an everyday occurrence.

The key thing about contract is that someone has identified a need and has also identified a thing of value to give to meet that need. The thing of value could differ from one person to another, it is a subjective situation.

We will in the illustrative scenes of this book role play contract principles while teaching you to think like a lawyer for your deals. Below are our two major characters:

Eve

Joe

OFFER

SCENE 1

It's a sunny, breezy and quiet afternoon at the Lagoon front. The blend of red and gold-coloured fabrics embellishing the raffia furniture livens the rather dreary mood of the relaxation centre popularly known to play host to many workers from nearby companies in busy noisy Victoria Island, Lagos. Seated in the corner, Joe, a fair complexioned lanky guy in his early 30s, seems to be in a world of his own, the empty chairs and quickly-melting iced cocktail being the reminder for him to return to work since break was over. He appears worried as if waiting for a guest. His growing tension transports his thoughts 5 years back to when he met her.

(Looking puzzled but at the same time wanting to be on top of the situation, Eve manages to respond)

Eve: Uhm, sure. We would send you our terms of engagement today. Once you sign off and make payment, we would come around tomorrow for the task.

Joe: Oh! I thought we already had a deal?

FLASHBACK

At Joe's office, D-Logistics Company representative, Eve, makes presentation on her company's range of services. Joe, looking obviously swayed responds.

Joe: Ok, "I think" I like your company's "offer", I accept every bit of it! There is a cargo to be moved. 6:30am tomorrow, please be prompt.

(Looking puzzled but at the same time wanting to be on top of the situation, Eve manages to respond)

Eve: Uhm, sure. We would send you our terms of engagement

today. Once you sign off and make payment, we would come around tomorrow for the task.

Joe: Oh! I thought we already had a deal?

PAUSE

Did you notice anything wrong? Is there an offer when a presentation is made to introduce the range of services that a company offers? Can you accept when there is no offer?

As trivial as the scenario looks, there are situations in business that call for real evaluation to ascertain whether there was an offer.

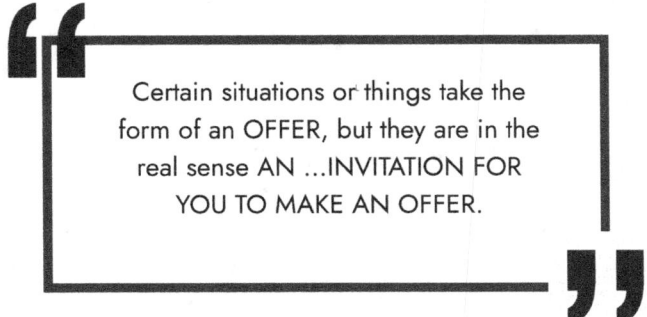

> Certain situations or things take the form of an OFFER, but they are in the real sense AN ...INVITATION FOR YOU TO MAKE AN OFFER.

There are situations where it looks like someone is making an offer, but in the real sense, the individual is asking you to make the offer. This situation is called INVITATION TO TREAT. That is, an invitation for you to make an offer.

An example is a pop-up advert by a furniture company for the sale of its product. Does the advert commit the company to sell or it establishes a basis for its customers to make an offer?

In answering this question, it is important to analyse the advert and then ask the question: "Did the company commit itself at any point?" That is why every situation must be looked at critically as there is no "one coat fits all" principle in law. The same principle is applicable to the conversation between Eve and Joe, the question is whether Eve committed her company at any point during the presentation.

Let us take a closer look at Joe's statement to see what we can learn:

Joe: "Ok, I think I like your company's offer, I accept every bit of it! "

There is a cargo to be moved. 6:30am tomorrow, please be prompt

ANALYSIS

Having analysed whether there was an offer or not. The second question is whether Joe's response is valid and capable of establishing a relationship? Before you say YES, remember, he was thinking and was not specific!

In business, there are times transactions are built on assumptions. Our law office handled a litigation for a contractor years ago. The company was in negotiation with a State Government for the construction of a commercial bridge and it deployed its resources to start work without a formal contract. They would have paid dearly for that costly assumption if not for the mediation panel that was set up to intervene later.

So, it is crucial to address transactions from what was communicated and not what is assumed.

When you see a prospective client thinking of making an offer, you can actually make the offer so that the client accepts or negotiates. Whichever way, you would have set the ball rolling.

Consider the alternative response below:

PLAY

Joe: Ok, great presentation. I have a cargo I desire to move by 6:30am tomorrow, what are your terms for the task?

PAUSE

What did you notice? Precision, accuracy, clarity and definitiveness.

Being accurate and precise means that you say what you mean and mean what you say. You must leave no room for exploitation which comes from ambiguous statements.

In business, you need to be precise as much as possible in communicating your offer. You should also understand your needs before you make an offer.

In other words, do not make an offer before understanding your needs because it could affect the negotiation.

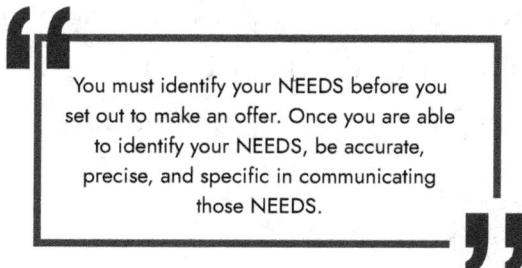

You must identify your NEEDS before you set out to make an offer. Once you are able to identify your NEEDS, be accurate, precise, and specific in communicating those NEEDS.

For Joe, his need is to have his cargo moved and the question is: what can he offer to have that need met?

As a teenager, one of the stories I enjoyed reading was that of the Bible characters- Esau and Jacob. In that story, Esau was the older brother and it had been foretold that Esau would serve Jacob, the younger. One day, Esau arrived home from the field and was "hungry to death", luckily, his brother, Jacob, just finished preparing stew, so Esau requested a portion of the meal. Jacob would have none of that. He had his mind set on all the rights that came with being a first born and he would rather have Esau give him those rights in exchange for stew. Esau was desperate for a meal at the time; he was too hungry, weak and tired to negotiate, so he caved in. Esau possibly thought that eating his brother's meal was the only option, but no. Let's look closely and identify options that could have led to a better deal for Esau:

a. Esau regularly comes home with harvests from the wild. His father loved him and he usually ate from his harvest. Could Esau have therefore told Jacob that he would give Jacob a portion of his harvest in exchange for a portion of Jacob's meal?

b. Could Esau have given Jacob a day's harvest and told Jacob to give his meal in exchange for his wild harvest?

The point is that people do not really take time to exhaust the many strengths, opportunities and options readily available to them before making an offer. People focus heavily on what they need and the situation they are in that they lose touch with what they have, is that you? It's time to start looking at the many available options.

Esau thought the best he could have was the meal from his brother, but he didn't consider a whole lot of areas he could offer value to get what he wanted and even more than he wanted.

Next, you should not think that one way always leads to the end. First reflect on the different areas and ways that you can offer value to get what you want.

I negotiated a settlement deal on behalf of a client some time ago. The parties on the other side owed my client and made a proposition to pay within a particular time frame. They would have made a better deal but they had a mental block that there was no way for them to get a better result.

First, they thought the offer they already made was the best they could afford to make and they also were too lazy to apply their minds to creatively think out alternative propositions. One of such would have been to negotiate for a cut if they were, by chance, able to pay within a shorter time, but they came to the negotiation table with a fixed mind that did not allow them to be creative in their propositions.

CAN AN OFFER BE MADE TO UNASCERTAINED PERSONS?

It is not uncommon to find offers being made to the public or a sector such that whoever meets the conditions is considered to have accepted the offer.

In this kind of situation, the person making the offer rarely knows the person who would accept that offer. This is why it is referred to as an offer to "unascertained persons" or a "general offer".

Can an offer be validly made to unascertained persons?

In answering the above question, you should remember that there is no hard and fast rule, so each case must be judged on its merit, and that you need to look at the peculiarities of your transaction.

The situation must be such that it is not an invitation to treat (that is, a call for the unascertained persons to make the offer). Our property subsidiary, for instance, would usually advertise openings in buildings that we manage for clients and also advertise those for sale. All of these adverts are directed towards unascertained people, but do they amount to an offer? Not necessarily, because those who see our adverts still come to negotiate terms with us until there is an agreement.

Let us take a look at the following instances:

FIRST ILLUSTRATION:

Invitation to Tender

Sealed tenders are invited from registered and reputable firms for the following services:

- Construction of underground drainage system
- Supply of drainage and general construction materials

Tender documents along with terms and conditions, date and time of tenders opening and tender evaluation forms can be downloaded from our website.

Management, APK Inc.

Can you say "YES, I have accepted?" No, because the invitation is preliminary to the ultimate offer. In essence, it is an invitation for you to make an offer.

SECOND ILLUSTRATION:

Advert to supply information and be entitled to a reward

Wanted: $5,000 reward for whereabouts of Bad Guy

There is a reward to anybody who can give information on the location of Bad Guy, he is wanted in connection with an attempted murder in Haven City.

Can you provide the information and claim the reward? Yes!

Why? Because it is A PROMISE FOR AN ACT.

That is "I promise to pay you $5,000 if you supply me with the whereabouts of Bad Guy.

SCENE 2

Joe relaxing at the Lagoon front during one of his work breaks. The location has become a reflection point for most of his business decisions. He sees a publication in a magazine he was reading. It is an invitation from Ivy Inc. to any African cocoa trader and exporter. Knowing he meets the requirements to make an offer, he quickly brings out his phone to document the necessary information he will need from the magazine. He pays for his drink and heads back to his office.

FADES

CROSS OFFER

SCENE 3

A Lady's bedroom...

The other parts of the room are dark except for the golden light from the lamp that spills on the legs of Eve; a beautiful young lady with an enchanting dimple that complements her glowing skin and long black hair carefully held in place by a hair net. She seems restless. She keeps turning on the bed reflecting on how business has brought Joe and her together and his request for friendship, picking up her phone and tossing it away. She finally picks up the courage to send a text to Joe.

Eve: "Hey Joe! I've been thinking about your friendship request. You approached me awkwardly, but it was very real and that got me attracted to you. I'm ready to be yours always- and seriously too. I accept to be your friend- friends for life."

Sends message and continues typing.

Almost immediately her phone shows: "Joe typing".

We hear the dual beep of Joe's inbox and Eve's delivery tone. The messages below were co-incidentally delivered on each recipient's phone:

Joe: "Oh my! You've just made my night! "Friends for life" is the plan. Can we meet after work tomorrow? I can't wait to see you."

Eve: 'If you would like, can we meet after work tomorrow to discuss this?

PAUSE

Both of them made a similar request to meet after work and the request co-incidentally delivered on each person's mobile device at the same time. Can there be a contract in the above situation?

What do you think?"

For there to be a contract, there must be at least one person to make an offer and another to accept. The kind of situation illustrated above is very remote, but it is not to say that it cannot happen.

Remember, there is no absolute answer for any situation especially in contractual relations. Each situation must be looked at contextually.

Here, you will find that there is a dual offer and no one to accept. The expression for the situation is called CROSS OFFER; that is, the offers were made coincidentally. Since, a contract is a product of offer and acceptance; it means that cross offer cannot lead to a contract.

In another sense, there was a precise offer but no unequivocal acceptance. In essence, the ingredients of a contract were not complete in the scenario.

So, there is no valid contract since there is a need for one person to make an offer and another to accept. The ideal thing will therefore be for either Eve or Joe to make the offer while the other accepts.

PLAY

Seeing their coincidental thought, Eve with a wide grin replies:

Eve: A sign that we will make good friends indeed. So, can we work towards meeting by 5pm at Oak and Spycee Restaulounge?

Joe (replying): Lol… a sign indeed. 5pm at the venue is fine by me. You know what, let me just give you a call. What are you doing now?"

FADES

COUNTER OFFER

Where a person "counters" an offer, his counter-proposal is said to become a COUNTER OFFER. What a Counter Offer does is that it aborts the original offer. In that sense, the person that made the initial offer becomes the one to accept what was counter-proposed.

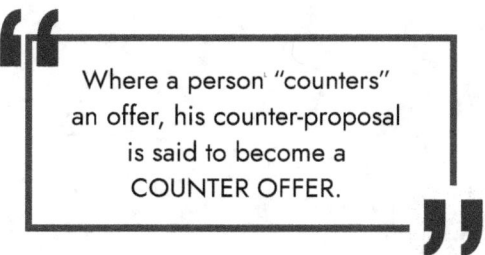

> Where a person "counters" an offer, his counter-proposal is said to become a COUNTER OFFER.

There are times when an offer goes back and forth; it could even become complicated to know who actually made the offer and who accepted. An example is the typical local market negotiation where both vendor and purchaser engage in a negotiation before settling for a final amount.

There are situations where a person's intention is to keep an offer open while seeking information to know whether the offer is good or not. Some time ago, our law firm negotiated the purchase of a large expanse of land for a client. The price and everything else were not a problem, but we needed to be sure that the land had government approvals. We could have simply responded to the offer by making our acceptance conditional on the land having government approval but knowing that it might amount to a counter-offer, we simply requested further information regarding the property and also made the seller know that our request for information was "without prejudice" to their offer.

SCENE 4

D-Logistics office complex. A large administrative building dominated by white walls that could not help but reflect the beautiful lighting. Eve, the company's representative is seen with a client -a man, making an offer to the company.

Eve: ... are there any other requests you would like to add sir?

Sam: No. That will be all for now. Please may I know your response to my offer so that I can know how to proceed with payment?

Eve was silent while looking through the notepad on her desk. She was not sure if the offer would be acceptable to her company or not. However, she wishes to keep the offer open to be able to discuss with her company to know if the offer is acceptable.

PAUSE

How do you think she should approach the situation?

Now, write your thoughts in the lines below:

_____

_____

_____

_____

_____

The first suggestion for her will be to as much as possible keep her conversations in writing because it is easier to prove than a verbal conversation. Then, she could let the prospective client know the ideal company's offer while emphasising that the information she shared is without any intention to overrule the prospective client's offer.

The expression used to represent this is WITHOUT PREJUDICE; it means that what is communicated should not be relied on in deciding legal rights.

PLAY

Eve: (After much thought) Alright Sir. I have written out your requests and will forward them to the board for consideration. Whatever response I get, I will make sure to communicate it to you. Nevertheless, please note that the information I have communicated is without prejudice to the board's decision.

Sam: Not a problem at all. Thank you very much Miss

Sam: Pardon me. (offering his hand) It was a pleasure talking with you. Do have a nice day.

Eve: (smiling) The pleasure is mine

FADES

While it is important to have the expression "without prejudice" stated in a conspicuous place in written correspondence, it is worth mentioning that the phrase "without prejudice" is not a magic wand. So, if during the negotiation you precisely and emphatically make an offer in reliance on which the other party is intended to act and does in fact act, you might be 'estopped' from claiming that your offer ought not to have been taken seriously. For instance, if Eve mentions to Sam that his offer is without prejudice to management's decision but then again ask him to make payment in line with his offer. If Sam relies on the instruction for him to pay and actually acted on it by making the payment, Eve and her company may be 'estopped' from contesting the validity of the agreement.

In a similar way, "without prejudice" does not mean that what you communicated cannot be revealed to a third party; it only means that it cannot be used to determine your legal rights and obligations.

TERMINATION OF OFFER

An offer may be brought to an end directly or indirectly. People sometimes assume that their offer is no longer on the table, but that assumption might be a costly one. Below are ways to end an offer and insightful principles for each situation.

REVOCATION: The word REVOKE means "cancel" and it is possible for an offer to be cancelled as long as the cancellation is communicated before acceptance.

Sometimes, revocation could be as a result of a substituted offer. We know of a client for instance who during the Covid-19 pandemic had to renegotiate pending offers made before the outbreak. With the attendant financial crisis that followed the pandemic, it was obvious to management that the company may go out of business if it did not renegotiate pending offers.

Lapse of time: Where an offer is not accepted within a period of time specified for acceptance, the offer would be deemed as being terminated once that time elapses.

Take for example that Sam requested for a response from D-Logistics Company within 3 days, if the company does not accept within 3 days that would amount to lapse of time.

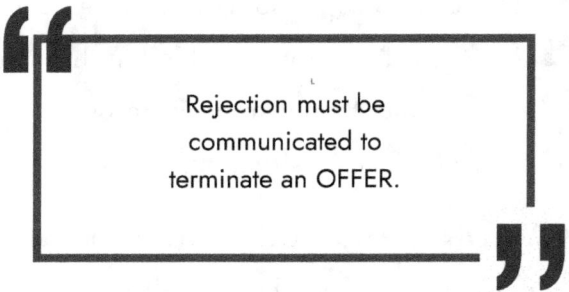

> Rejection must be communicated to terminate an OFFER.

There are situations where the urgency of time is not stated but may be reasonably inferred from an offer. For instance, a cake craft company that receives an offer to make cake for an event cannot seek to accept the offer after the event.

REJECTION OR COUNTER OFFER: Where d-logistics communicate its rejection of Sam's offer or alters the offer in any way as to place a new offer on the table, Sam's offer stands terminated.

This plays out a great deal during negotiations; people usually have moments where they try to agree on what is expected and the price in the course of which multiple offers spring out of the same transaction.

During the course of writing this book for instance, I had to negotiate with a user interface (UI) developer to help with the design of a web project I co-founded. He made an initial offer of $700, I offered part payment in cash and another part by way of legal service, he turned down my offer and made another offer for $500, I pushed further for the same offer and then he made a final offer of $500 but with a more flexible payment plan.

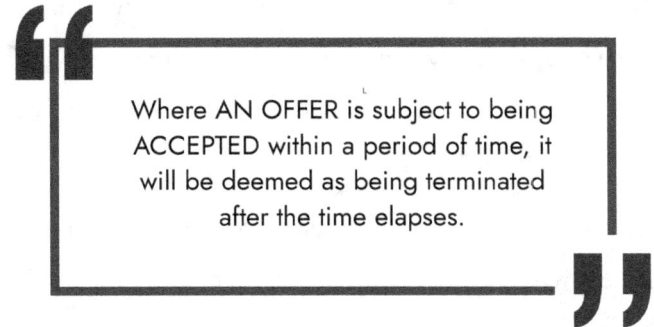

> Where AN OFFER is subject to being ACCEPTED within a period of time, it will be deemed as being terminated after the time elapses.

As minute as the negotiation is, it represents what happens

while trying to broker deals such that it might even become dicey to figure out who eventually made the ultimate offer and who accepted.

One more thing- rejection must be communicated to terminate an offer.

DEATH

Where Sam passed away, the offer will be terminated.

However, this may not be the case in all situations.

In a stricter sense of AN AGREEMENT, what if a person or an entity accepts the offer of another before finding out about the death of the person or that entity?

Death can abort both an offer and a contract depending on the situation. Going by the rule of judging every situation on its merit, you might have discovered that there is absolutely no right response as the response depends on the situation and the express terms of the contract.

For instance, where a person accepts the offer of another before knowing about the other person's demise, what happens?

Let's say Mr. Do Good of Do Good Inc. made an offer to Ben on behalf of Do Good Inc. and then Ben dies. What do you think of this situation?

It depends on the nature of the contract; was the offer made in particular, to Ben and in expectation of Ben's expertise or is it such that can be done by another?

Below are illustrations:

1. What happens where Dave, a lawyer offers to prepare an agreement in his private capacity but dies and the client finds out about his demise after accepting to give the job to him? the deal is terminated because it is an offer for a professional service which is personal to the lawyer.

2. What happens where IVY INC. makes an offer to joe investments limited (SJIL) and SJIL communicates that it accepts the offer without knowing that Tom (CEO of Ivy Inc.) died shortly after the offer was communicated?

The deal remains valid because IVY INC. is an artificial person in the eyes of the law and has a legal personality distinct from its CEO, Mr. Tom.

ACCEPTANCE

SCENE 5

It is mid-day and Joe is seen chilling at the lagoon front. He reflects on the publication that he saw in the magazine the other day. Lost in thought and trying to figure how to write an appealing offer, the ringtone from Joe's phone brings his thoughts back to the present. We hear the voice of a lady over the phone. After some minutes, he hangs up with a bright face and looks towards an open path where Genie makes her way towards him. With a wide smile, Joe gives her a warm embrace while offering her a seat. Without further delay, the following conversation ensued:

Joe: You know, it's been five years that you have rendered legal support services to our company. All through the years, you have helped us to make the right decisions and also avoid catastrophic *mistakes. I want us to take the relationship to the next level. Genie, will you be our company secretary?*

Genie: (obviously taken aback) Oh my! I am not quite sure how to respond here Joe! Thank you for commending my efforts, but... But...Erm... I don't think I'm ready to quit active law practice... Can you give me some time? Maybe another two years? I really need to be ready for this.

Let's hold it there!

QUESTION: Has Genie accepted Joe's offer in that situation? If YES, how? And If NO, how come?

Now, write your thoughts in the lines below:

_____

_____

_____

_____

_____

_____

Let us analyse the situation:

First, did you notice Genie brought in something in addition to the offer? (that is, the request for them to wait for another two years)

You might say, "But then, her response shows that she is interested!"

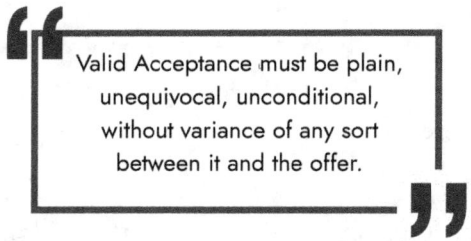

> Valid Acceptance must be plain, unequivocal, unconditional, without variance of any sort between it and the offer.

That is not sufficient! Acceptance has to be an unequivocal concession to what was presented as the offer. Imagine a car dealer offers you a car for 3500USD but you requested to pay 2500USD. What would be the status of the initial offer for 3500USD? The request to pay 2500USD is a new offer.

What that new offer does is that it kills the original offer, so Genie cannot hold Joe accountable for his offer when she already made another offer.

In essence, valid Acceptance has to be plain, unequivocal, unconditional, without variance of any sort between it and the offer.

At the time of publishing this book, one of my executive students got an offer to install window blinds. Everything about the offer appeared favourable except that her client requested to pay for the entire service after installation which did not go down well with her; she wanted payment before service. As a result of this, she made adjustments to the offer which included that her client gives a post-dated cheque. At that point, she became the one making an offer and her client's duty was to either accept or reject. If he had rejected the offer, she could not have revisited the initial offer made by the client with the intention of accepting it because that was forfeited by reason of her new offer.

Similarly, acceptance may be inferred from the recipient's conduct. For instance, if Genie begins to resume and act the role of a company secretary in line with Joe's offer, it might be reasonable to infer that Genie accepted Joe's offer, especially because she has altered her daily engagements to suit the offer.

Finally, acceptance must be communicated within a reasonable time frame if time is of importance. If Joe, for instance, had told Genie, "we need a company secretary within the next 6 months?" Genie cannot seek to accept the offer in the 7th month because Joe had added a time factor to his offer.

If it may be reasonably inferred that "time" is of importance from the nature of an offer, then that offer ought to be accepted within a reasonable time frame.

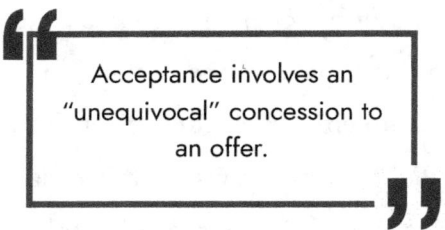

I was a part of a negotiation team that received an offer to construct a local market which the local government authority planned to launch at its upcoming memorial event.

Although, nothing was said about the need to either accept or reject the offer within a time frame, we knew that we ought to give a YES or NO soon enough since the contract itself must be completed before the event.

What if the person to whom an offer was made was not aware of the offer? What do you think? Highlight your thoughts below:

_____

_____

_____

_____

_____

SCENE 6

Eve: (touching his pensive face) I'm so sorry Darl. You should have told me earlier when I thought I was old enough to marry (speaking sarcastically).

Joe: (joining the rhetoric but meaning what he said) Well, I did. I mailed you some months ago to ask for your hand in marriage. I wanted you to bring it up, to talk about it but you never did. I thought you weren't okay with the email proposal.

Eve: Oh my! I'm so sorry Joe. Okay, Okay, erm… I don't even know what I am thinking. Look Joe, I haven't seen your mail (do I even want to see it?). Whatever is there, I have heard and I accept....

Joe: Really? Can you accept an offer that you have not seen? Hahaha!

PAUSE

The point is that you cannot accept an offer that you are not aware of.

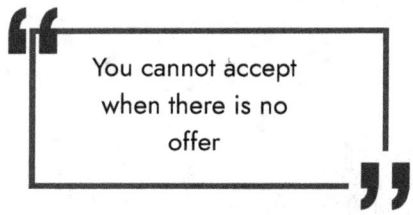

However, once you are aware of an offer, your motive or intention for accepting does not matter. So, if there is an offer to pay 1000USD to anyone that can give the police information that would lead to the arrest of Mr. Bad Guy, if Nice Guy decides to give the information because he has bitter rivalry with Bad Guy, it would not stop Nice Guy from claiming the prize.

You cannot ACCEPT when there is no OFFER

So, you will find in conclusion that a contract is a product of the combination of OFFER and ACCEPTANCE and that it could be written, oral, or implied by conduct.

CONSIDERATION

As earlier mentioned, contract is about identifying and meeting needs. The question that you need to answer when you set out to do a deal is WHAT AM I CONSIDERING TO GIVE to get what I want?

To have a great time negotiating, you should have a hint of what will appeal to the person on the other side of the table and that is what should eventually guide your negotiation.

So, Joe could ask himself for instance:

Basis of Contract

What do I want?

What am I willing to give to get what I want?

Every consideration must be a thing of value to the person at the other end. It does not have to make sense to you, as far as it does to the person you are dealing with. In essence, the word "thing of value" is relative and in the absence of fraud, duress, misrepresentation and other vitiating factors, a contract is valid no matter how intangible a consideration seems. We have brokered a lot of property deals for clients that some looked unreal either because the seller was seemingly selling at a ridiculously cheap price, or the buyer was paying an outrageously high amount.

Many people have even gifted things of value away. The position of the law is that consideration needs not be adequate but it must be sufficient (in essence, the question is NOT whether a good deal has been struck, but whether a thing of value no matter how intangible has been given). "Clearance sales" is an example of an instance where prices drop. That the seller made a personal choice to reduce price such that the price is unreasonable will not invalidate sales. Transactions hinge on subjective test because of the assumption that we are social beings with liberty to make decisions and be bound by those decisions.

Is it possible that only one party intends to give a thing of value? Yes, it is. Such a contract is best put in written form (preferably by deed). The word "deed" is not a magic wand; a written agreement that is titled as a "Deed" and signed may be qualified to be called a contract by deed. E.g. Deed of Gift. If it therefore happens that you would receive something free without giving anything in return, you should have the deal spelt out in a document and signed by the giver.

Some years ago, my daughter was gifted with acres of land.

The giver signed a Deed of Gift to make the transfer to her. Wills and codicils are other documents used to gift things. You will find that they are usually in written form. It is a hectic exercise to start an oral transaction where only one party intends to give something to another party and that other party has no obligation to reciprocate.

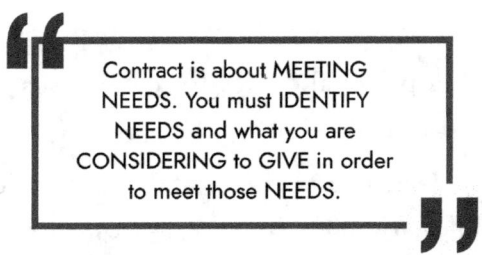

> Contract is about MEETING NEEDS. You must IDENTIFY NEEDS and what you are CONSIDERING to GIVE in order to meet those NEEDS.

Sometimes too, something of value may be done or given voluntarily without being reciprocated by the recipient. If the recipient after receiving value, decides independently to reciprocate, that decision cannot be validly enforced. In this situation, the recipient may not be validly sued for the pledge since it was made after receiving the thing of value.

Sometime ago, a colleague from our Firm went for a negotiation meeting on behalf of one of our clients. We negotiated with a taxi driver to take her to and fro the meeting. The deal was sealed and payments made. However, the meeting went on till late in the day such that both of them did not make it back until much later than anticipated. My colleague had a nice time on the trip, loved the driver's attitude and therefore promised to compensate him with an additional amount. Can the rider enforce that promise in court? Maybe not, because it was made independently of the contract with our Firm and the driver has an existing duty to drive her back to the office.

The summary here is that performance of an existing duty does not amount to consideration.

Many artisans have a trend of undertaking to do things without negotiating the cost. Legally speaking, such situations might land them in trouble because a recipient that refuses to pay may not be validly sued for that decision except it can be demonstrated that there is some form of understanding that payment would be made for the service.

For instance, Greg, a laptop engineer undertakes to fix Jade's laptop without any promise of payment by Jade. Just after fixing the laptop, a grateful Jade promises to pay Greg $50 but reneges on paying, Greg may not be able to claim the sum because the promise was not the basis of the repairs done by Greg.

The summary therefore is that something already done in the past, given or promised cannot be used as consideration for an extant contract.

INTENTIONS IN RELATIONSHIPS

PLAY

SCENE 7

(At Oak and Spycee Restaulounge)

Eve: I love this ambience; it is gradually becoming my best meal spot. What if we visit on a regular basis? (amused)

PAUSE

Certain conversations do not necessarily lead to a relationship that can be enforced in court. A good example is an informal gesture which parties do not reasonably intend would lead to a legally binding relationship. Such gestures might create a moral obligation which is enforceable only in the court of conscience and morality (if there is anything like that).

Moral relations happen across different contexts especially social and domestic relationships. The presumption is that agreements entered into between people in a social or domestic relationship is not enforceable unless it can first be established that there was an intention for the agreement to be enforceable. So, if Joe agrees to take Eve to Oak and Spycee on a regular basis, she may not be able to enforce it in court if he fails on the agreement.

Conversely, the intention to create legally binding relations is presumed in commercial agreements such that it is the person claiming lack of intention that has the task of establishing the assertion. The same principle applies in agreements between corporate entities due to the presumption that blood and emotions do not flow through the veins of corporate entities. One of the rationales for the presumption here is the need to have a regulated society that ensures parties are bound by their promises.

Where a commercial agreement is to be started but not intended to be enforceable, it has to be expressly stated in the agreement, otherwise the context must clearly establish the intentions.

A lack of intention to create legal relations does not mean a contract isn't in existence. Rather, it means that the contract may not be enforceable through the courts. Sympathisers may mount pressure to enforce the deal, but the courts will not interfere. So, if I promise my daughter a vacation trip if she learns how to make cake and she eventually learns but I renege on my promise, her mother may persuade me to fulfil my promise but she may not be able to sue me in court for breach of contract. That is because if the courts were to enforce this kind of situation, it would lead to a floodgate of litigation and human relationships would be irreparably damaged.

There is a general presumption against an intention to create legal relation in contracts between parents, spouses, siblings and close peers. Such relationships are called "social and domestic contracts". It does not however mean that there cannot be a valid contract between people in a social or domestic relation. The question is "did the parties intend to create legal relations?"

"Context" is essential in determining if there is an intention to create legal relations or not and parties must reasonably know or agree that if anything goes wrong, they may be sued in court. For instance, where parties in social relations agree to do a purely commercial transaction, the presumption against intention to create legal relations may be said to have been rebutted.

If you intend to start an agreement with someone within your social or domestic network and you want it to be binding, it might help to have the agreement in written form clearly stating all terms and conditions including the fact that parties intend the agreement to be binding and enforceable.

SITUATIONS OF INVALID CONTRACT ENTRY

Once people start a contract freely with mutual assent, they owe a duty to themselves to honour their individual obligations under the contract. In legal sense, this is referred to as the doctrine of "sanctity of contract".

The basis of punishment for refusal to honour contract obligations stems from the presumption that the defaulter must have intended to enter a legally binding relationship and ought to be responsible for any action or inaction that falls short of the contractual obligations.

There are however situations that may impair the validity of a contract such that the relationship may be put to an end or even unenforceable. Below are some examples of those instances:

- Misrepresentation: a person mentioned something to another person as true which that other person later discovers to be untrue. In this kind of situation, the untrue statement must have been the basis for entering into the relationship.

- Mistake: the relationship itself was founded on error.

- Duress: there was an element of coercion or force which made a person to enter a relationship. In essence, the element of "voluntariness" which is key to a valid contract is missing.

- Undue Influence: there was some form of pressure from someone whom the other person holds in high esteem by reason of which the contract was not voluntarily entered into.

You will notice that "undue influence" is closely related to "duress". One of the key differences is that there is usually a relationship factor in "undue influence" and the decision to start the contract is usually as a result of the person who is held in high esteem. Also, a relationship may exist in the situation of duress but the decision to start a contract in the case of duress is usually fueled by some form of coercion like force, undue pressure, violence or threat.

- Illegality: the entire agreement is built on something that is wrongful by law.

Now, let's take a closer look at these terms to have a deeper understanding of how they affect deals.

MISREPRESENTATION

Contracts are a product of words- whether written or verbal. The word "misrepresentation" stems from the word "represent" which means that someone said (represented) something to someone else. When what was said is false, the word "mis" is added and the situation is referred to as a "misrepresentation". The representation may be made by a third party who is not a party to the contract. In that situation, the extent of relationship with the third party may be a factor in determining whether the contract is valid or not.

It is important to look at the context of what was said and see also that the person that it was communicated to relied on it to start the contract. When that is the case, the person who was misled may be entitled to some form of remedy.

For instance, I ordered window blinds for my apartment around the period of writing this chapter. I wanted the windows to have a new look and give the house new ambience too. I had the option of buying cheaper stocks but I chose to make the more expensive order because I was convinced by the seller about the quality of her blinds. If the seller had asserted that her blinds do not peel, and I rested on her statement to make a purchase, that might amount to a warranty and I may be able to claim compensation if what was said turned out to be false.

When someone says what he or she thinks, that might not be a misrepresentation because that is just an opinion. One of the ways to differentiate is to analyse what was said and how it was said and then ask if it reasonably induced the other party to start the contract.

When a statement is made as an opinion, you have a duty to make personal findings and not go on to strike a deal based on the statement. So, a person who merely said she believes that backyard farm produce is better than farmland produce may be saying it as an opinion.

Sometimes too, in transactions, certain points are innocently mentioned without intention to lure the other party into contract and those words turn out false. Does the other party have a right especially where the misrepresentation was the basis of starting the contract? Yes, the person may pull out without having the right to seek compensation (except where the person can prove loss as a result of the wrong information).

If you assert a point without believing it to be true and that point makes the other person start a contract with you, then, that may amount to negligent misrepresentation.

Your position at the point of making the statement matters especially where you owe a duty of care to the person to whom you made the untrue statement.

It is common for people to start a contract as a result of an untrue statement made by the other party. It is also common that once the untrue statement is discovered, many people try to pull through in the contract thereby condoning the misrepresentation. You must know when to pull the trigger and when to bury the hatchets as a deal maker seeking to use the knowledge of the law to your advantage.

Here are thoughts on misrepresentation:

■ For a statement to be a misrepresentation, it must have been communicated prior to when a contract was formed.

■ The aim of such statements most times is to induce the other person to enter a contract.

■ The statement must have been untrue to the knowledge of the maker. Sometimes, someone that makes an untrue statement might believe in the truth of the statement, the person would still be liable if it is unreasonable or careless for the maker to have thought that the statement was true.

■ A statement may be an oral communication, an act or even inaction. It usually does not matter if the statement is a half-truth. Once there is an element of falsity in the statement which was the basis of accepting the contract, then, it might amount to a misrepresentation.

■ The receiver of the statement must have relied on the statement to start a contract with the person who made the statement.

What if the person who made the false statement was a third party? For instance, Joe spoke very highly about his friend; Texas to lure Ivy Inc. into a business relationship, even though those things he said about Texas were unverified. What are your thoughts in that scenario? You should be careful with third party statements. Where you are to act on them, ensure that the third party makes an undertaking to cover any liability that may arise as a result of your reliance on the statement. Otherwise, you should take time to do your checks to confirm the truth or otherwise of the statement.

■ In the case of a misrepresentation, the misled party may be entitled to exit the contract, request for compensation, opt to carry on with the contract, have terms adjusted or renegotiated, etc.

SCENE 8

Joe's friend, Texas, an ambitious and fairly successful entrepreneur has a keen interest in growing his cashew business from local supplies to exportation.

Joe, who has a good rapport with Ivy Inc decides to introduce Texas to the company and misled the company into believing that Texas is a well-established cashew exporter. Ivy Inc. accepted to start a relationship with Texas solely because of the statement made by Joe.

What do you think?

Is there a contract?

Write your thoughts in the lines below:

MISTAKE

It is common for people to talk about "mistake" in the general sense of something that happened without intent and then rest on it as a defence. Does this match with the legal sense of the word and its consequences? Maybe not!

To think like a lawyer, you need to understand what qualifies as a mistake in the legal sense. A business executive that signs an agreement thinking she was signing another document might claim a mistake, but not a driver that breaks the speed limit even though he did not intend to do so.

In essence, a mistake of the law is no excuse.

You cannot by reason of ignorance of what the law states, say you made a "mistake". The maxim is that ignorance of the law is not an excuse. In essence, your mistake about what the law states about a transaction is not sufficient excuse for you to seek to nullify that transaction.

For instance, you intended to buy a piece of land in a residential area but you did not know that the land you were purchasing was already earmarked under the town planning law as an industrial area and then you made a purchase. After sealing the deal, you wanted to build and market for sale, but found out that the land was not suitable and the fact about your intention were not known to the seller prior to when the deal was sealed, you thought you bought cheap but now see the purchase was not worth it. These facts may not be sufficient to nullify the transaction particularly when what you intended to do with the land was not a precondition to the purchase. This is also why it may help to be as open as possible with your contracts.

One of the ways to overcome the hurdle of mistake of law is for you to have clauses in your agreement that protects your intentions and everything you want to do from the factual situation.

The illustration above is a typical example of a unilateral mistake. A unilateral mistake may sometimes not be a basis to validly let go of a contract except it can be demonstrated by the complainant that the other party prompted the mistake and perhaps, also had knowledge of the other person's error or is in position to reasonably know that the other person was acting in error.

There are also mutual mistakes. Here, all parties must have had false assumptions which formed the basis of the contract. Parties can let go of the relationship at that point except if they mutually want to embrace the contract notwithstanding the mistake.

There could be common errors about the same subject matter. An example is a situation where people that seek to start a contract thought the subject matter of the contract was in existence when it was not. The contract may be nullified in that instance.

Another instance is where the parties to a contract intended a contract but are mutually at cross-purpose about some material facts relating to the contract. For instance, A wanted to buy armless chairs from B, they spoke on the phone and seemed to be in understanding about the contract, but B mistook A's purchase offer for $3 per chair while A thought that B requested to purchase 24pieces. In essence, A's offer was misinterpreted while B also had misconception. So, here, the issue is that there could not be an offer in the absence of agreement as to the same thing. This situation is called MUTUAL MISTAKE and parties may opt to renegotiate terms in order to agree on the same thing.

It has been said often that "if you want to hide something from someone, hide it in an agreement because some people do not read before they sign". In this age of digitalisation and tech-enablement where terms and conditions may come in electronic form, you need to spend time reading especially platforms and transactions that matter because the rule is stricter in relationships built on documents and you may not say that you were in mistake of a transaction just because you did not read and therefore thought you were signing something else (i.e. non- est factum). You cannot say your assent was not your deed, unless you can prove fraud, misrepresentation or other defences to show that the other party lured or deliberately intended to defraud you.

A good basis for non-est factum is where a party happens to be an illiterate. The word "illiterate" does not mean that a person is not schooled. Rather, it means the person is not in a position to understand the language in which a transaction was presented. If this can be proved, the person may be exempted from any liability.

If you are dealing with people that do not understand the language of a transaction or are blind and therefore unable to read. To protect yourself, you must ensure that someone else interprets or reads out the document and the person confirms that the content is clear after which the interpreter signs at the end of the Agreement that the document has been translated or read out in a language that the illiterate understands and that it was after the illiterate seemed to have clearly understood the document that the illiterate signed it. The entire portion that deals with that is otherwise known as an illiterate jurat and below is an example:

The content of this Agreement was read to the Purchaser and interpreted from English to French Language by me, Jack Joe of 112 Price Water Avenue, North London, United Kingdom after which the Purchaser signed when he appeared to have perfectly understood the content of the Agreement.

If a party is illiterate by virtue of being blind, an illiterate jurat may state as follows:

The content of this Agreement was read aloud and interpreted from English to French Language by me, Jack Joe of 112 Price Water Avenue, North London, United Kingdom after which the Purchaser signed when he appeared to have perfectly understood the content of the Agreement

Interestingly, these days there are devices that can be used to interpret documents. The relevance of having an illiterate jurat in agreement may therefore begin to dwindle. Nevertheless, it may be safer to have an illiterate jurat for many reasons including the fact that translating machines and devices may be automated and not necessarily perfect in all ways.

In summary, if you sign a document without reading it, it might amount to negligence and the excuse of signing in error may not be available.

DURESS

As stated earlier, the basis of contract is that parties voluntarily entered into an agreement. One of the reasons that contracts may not be enforceable is in the situation of duress. Duress involves a situation where a person uses varying degrees of threat to persuade another to start a contract. In that situation, the contract is voidable by the victim.

In determining what amounts to pressure, there is need to show that the victim's freewill was undermined by unfair pressure or threat. So, the contract must have been induced by improper threat and the victim must have had little or no choice but to enter the contract as a result of the threat.

The victim has a right to carry on with the contract or withdraw from it.

Certain threats may not necessarily amount to duress. One of such is where the alleged threat is a result of a factual situation.

As a business advisory firm, we have brokered many settlement deals for clients. Some of those deals started by way of letter threatening legal action. Most times, the threatened party usually opts for a settlement deal **because the threat is a result of factual situation.** Can the threatened party renege on such settlement contracts on the basis of threat of legal action? Not necessarily, because the clients we acted for were within their legal right to threaten legal action.

The focus is not that there was a threat, rather, the focus is that the threat affected the state of mind of the victim. If the victim's position in life is such that they ought not to have been affected by the threat, then, it may not amount to duress. For instance, if a rookie threatened to punch a heavyweight boxer if he does not sign a contract, that may not amount to duress since the boxer is a professional who should hardly be threatened by such a confrontation.

In contrast, our Firm handled the case of a client who lost his job due to the economic impact of a global pandemic, his former employers seized his car and threatened to immediately put it on sale if he did not sign an agreement to repay the outstanding car loan as scheduled in his payment plan while in their employment. The validity of the agreement was challenged on the basis of duress and the fact that the client was most likely going to be without a job for a while, so the chances of default was going to be high.

Situations might also arise during negotiation where a party uses information to their advantage against the other party. Sometime ago, I was engaged to negotiate the sale of an expanse of land within Lagos, Nigeria. The property had a valuation of 15m per plot, however, we did a hard bargaining down to 3m per plot for one reason- we knew that the vendor desperately needed the money to pay his indebtedness to a local bank and it would be hard for the vendor to get a single purchaser for value to purchase the entire property.

The test of a reasonable person is crucial in determining what amounts to duress. In essence, if the situation is such that a reasonable person in the victim's shoes may not have succumbed to the threat, then the situation may not be considered as a threat. The same thing applies when, reasonably speaking, the victim could have taken advantage of some alternative options. In that situation, the claim for duress may not avail the victim.

SCENE 9

The Joes' house. Joe and Eve are having breakfast.

Joe: This food is superb! I intend to start "Alone in the Kitchen Series" for men who want to learn culinary skills.

Eve: (speaking humourously) What! Joe in the kitchen? Hahaha!

Joe: There she goes again. Never mind, your husband is a super-duper cook.

Eve: Oh, you mean like a duper? (both laugh)

Joe: (Holding her hand) Thanks for the meal.

Eve: You're welcome. You owe me anyway. Yea…That reminds me. How was your meeting with the supplier, did he agree to your proposal?

Joe: (soberly speaking) No, he did not. We were at logger-heads. He said he wouldn't agree to my offer unless I doubled the actual price. He knows I need the goods badly and things are very scarce these days (rising and reaching for his bag), I really need to leave now I don't want to be late.

Eve: Hmmm! Do take care. I will talk to you later in the day for updates. (kisses him as he heads for the door)

FADES

If Joe goes ahead to sign a contract with the supplier, can he rely on the defense of duress?

What do you think? Will the contract be valid?

Write your thoughts in the lines below:

_____

_____

_____

_____

_____

UNDUE INFLUENCE

As stated earlier, one easy way to learn "legal terms" is to first view them as mere English words. "Undue" as a word means a situation that was unwarranted, unnecessary, unjustified, uncalled for, etc. To "Influence" means to impart, inspire, induce, etc. You will therefore notice an emotional play.

Where a person takes undue advantage of another person as a result of an existing relationship, this may amount to a contract entered under undue influence. Conversely, a person that starts a contract as a result of improper pressure may be said to have been unduly influenced.

In situations of undue influence, it is typical to see someone exploiting a relationship for gain while the other person is under pressure in the relationship to their loss.

Typical examples of situations that may lead to undue influence are; doctor-patient relationships, lawyer-client relationships, teacher-student relationship, etc. You will notice that those relationships are a product of a high reference, trust and respect by one party for the other such that it might be easy for the trusted person to abuse position to make undue gain. The concept of undue influence is therefore to protect the vulnerable from exploitation by the more powerful party.

While "undue influence" occurs more in transactions between individuals, it may not be easily relied on in transactions involving companies because companies are usually independent of their founders and directors and cannot be said to have emotions that can be taken undue advantage of.

ILLEGALITY

When a contract involves an act that is not allowed by law or against public policy (including public acceptance), it may amount to an illegal contract.

A contract may be illegal because of its formation, performance or both.

A transaction was brokered between a company and one of the banks of that period. Both parties agreed to secure the overdraft with a property belonging to the estate of a deceased and the deceased was made the guarantor. The bank had a foreknowledge that the person being presented as a guarantor was deceased at the time of the transaction and was therefore unable to enforce the contract and its breach.

You may ask, "Why would the bank be unable to enforce the contract between the company and the bank?"

The answer is that the formation of the agreement was built on an illegality (i.e. contract with a deceased person).

A contract may validly go through the process of negotiation, offer, acceptance and consideration. However, the contract may not be capable of being enforced if the subject of agreement or a part of it is illegal or violates public policy.

So, if "X" enters an agreement with a clearing agent to clear a consignment which contains a box of illegal substance and some laptops, the entire contract might become unenforceable by reason of the illegal consignment.

Sometimes, the reason a contract becomes illegal may be because of its consequence on people that are not part of the contract.

Courts will often not enforce illegal contracts because of the need for public deterrence or where a law provides that such contract cannot be enforced.

If you partake in an illegal contract, chances are that it may be hard for you to reclaim anything in it. That is why it is often said that "there is no honour among thieves". However, if you were misled into an illegal contract, you may be able to bring the relationship to an end and claim your principal investments. You may however need to prove that there is little or no way for you to have known of the illegality of the contract.

SCENE 10

Later in the day. Joe drives into the office complex as Charles, a young budding entrepreneur whose office is a cubicle away from Joe walks up to him for some advice.

Charles: Hi Joe, what's up this morning?

Joe: Up? The sky is blue! (chuckles softly)

Charles: Got some minutes to spare? I need your advice on something.

Joe: Not a problem. What is it?

Charles: There was this friend of mine who linked me to a business. I was engaged to clear a consignment which I agreed to but later discovered it contains a box of illegal substance and some laptops. I don't know what to do because I don't want to be involved in illegal business and I have already signed the contract without knowing.

Joe: Really? *(looking shocked)* Have you considered pulling out of the transaction?

Charles: I thought so too, but what if they sue me? One needs a fat purse to get a good lawyer

Joe: Maybe not. Look, I think you should pull out of that deal. If anything happens, just let me know and I will see what I can do to help.

Charles: No problem Joe, thanks for always being there.

Joe: Anytime. *(walks into the office building)*

PAUSE

BASIC POINTS TO CONSIDER BEFORE THE CONTRACT

Healthy relationships have something in common- TRUST. With trust comes a sense of SECURITY so that no one feels agitated, afraid or burdened.

That there is TRUST does not mean that the parties are unguarded or that the relationship is guarded by reckless decisions clouded by emotions. Rather, the ideal healthy relationship is the one that has palliative measures in place to help every aspect of the parties' relationship.

For Joe to want to go into a business relationship with Ivy Inc, he is presumed to at least know the name of the company he wants to do business with, he needs to be clear about his decision to start the deal with the company (sometimes things do not go smoothly but people do not ordinarily go into deals to not make it work), he needs to have the idea of what each person should do to make the relationship work and he must have his expectations about Ivy Inc's capacity at playing its roles too.

The same thing is applicable to Ivy Inc. The company would expect nothing less for it to start the business relationship.

While the assumptions above do not guarantee that Joe's company and Ivy Inc. will have a never-ending relationship, they at least give each of them a reason to show commitment in the relationship. That is how deals also ought to be made.

In business, every person trying to seal a deal and those reflecting on whether to accept or reject are faced with a similar issue of insecurity. One of the ways to deal with it is to identify the areas of concern and then introduce protective and reassuring points as part of the Agreement. We negotiated a joint venture on behalf of a client with a Chinese national, and even though the Chinese was represented by a lawyer considered competent in all ways, we had a protracted time negotiating because the Chinese national kept coming up with "what ifs". One would easily notice that he was insecure and therefore needed guidance from his lawyer.

Depending on the kind of relationship, below is an excerpt of standard points that you should consider in your Agreement:

1. Identified parties
2. Clearly spelt out reason for the relationship
3. Role playing
4. Duration of relationship
5. Incentives from relationship
6. Deterrence for wrong doing
7. Conflict management measures

Identified Parties

The basis of identity is to know who each person is. Care should be taken to ensure that full names are shared together with traceable addresses. The same principle is applicable to companies; you need to check the archive of the commission in charge of registering companies to find out the registered name and address of the company. An example of a clause identifying a party is stated below:

> "Ivy Inc. of 46 West 51st Street, New York City, NY 10036, U.S.A."

Clearly spelt out reason for the relationship

Here is where the intention of each person as well as the basis of the contract is stated. A well spelt out intention prepares everybody to understand their roles in the relationship. Below is an example:

> "Ivy Inc. desires to import cocoa seeds from Africa and Joe has the know-how to source and export cocoa seeds from any part of Africa to Europe"

Role Playing

As mentioned earlier, a person that sets out to start a relationship must ask the questions "what do I want from this relationship" and "what am I willing to give to get what I want?" The basis of role play in any relationship is that the people in the relationship have identified what they each want and what they intend to give to get what they want.

As explained earlier, the thing of value that each person wants from a relationship may differ, what therefore matters is that the value is fair in the eyes of the person entering the relationship. Below is an example of a simple role play clause:

> "Ivy Inc. has agreed to pay the sum of $250 to Joe as consideration for his undertaking to source and export cocoa seeds from Africa to Europe for Ivy Inc."

Observe how the role play flows from the reason for the relationship.

Duration of relationship

When time matters in a relationship, it may be important to mention when the relationship is to start and when it is supposed to end. Where time is of essence, it becomes a breach if a party is unable to conclude obligations before the agreed time. Below are examples:

> "Joe agrees to source for and export cocoa seeds to Ivy Inc. within two weeks of receiving the sum of $250 from Ivy Inc."

> "This Agreement will exist from the period when parties sign until Joe sources for and exports cocoa seed to Ivy Inc."

You might ask the question, "what happens if a party does not perform its obligation on time?" It is not in all situations that missing a contractual deadline will amount to a serious breach. There will therefore be a need to answer the question- "how serious is the breach?" and the most important consideration, in answering that question, is the subject of contract. A person that agrees to transport fresh tomatoes within seven days but delays by a day may be said to be in serious breach considering that the subject of contract is perishable. However, a contractor that agrees to finish a building project within five months but finishes in the sixth month may not be said to be in material breach.

One of the tools that can be used to communicate the importance of time in a contract is the "time is of essence" clause. If time is of the essence in performing a contractual obligation, you need to ensure that it is clearly stated in the Agreement. Conversely, where you find it stated in a contract that time is of the essence, you need to ensure that you perform your role within the stipulated time. A sample clause is provided below:

> "Parties agree that time is of the essence in performing their respective obligations"

Incentives from relationship

"Incentives" refer to the rewards from a relationship. Sometimes, the rewards may be interwoven or stated together with the role play and sometimes, it may be separately stated. Below are examples for the two instances:

> "Ivy Inc. has agreed to pay the sum of $250 to Joe as consideration for his undertaking to source and export cocoa seeds from Africa to Europe for Ivy Inc."

NOTE: The reward to Joe is the $250 while the reward to Ivy Inc. is the cocoa seeds.

However, where the reward is to be stated differently, it could be something like this:

"Ivy Inc. has agreed to mobilise Joe and Joe has agreed to source and export seeds from Africa to Europe for Ivy Inc. on the following basis:

Incentives:

> 1. Ivy Inc. agrees to pay the sum of $250 to Joe as full payment for him to source and export

cocoa seeds from Africa to Ivy Inc.'s factory at 46 West 51st Street, New York City, NY 10036, U.S.A.

2. Joe agrees to deliver the cocoa seeds on or before 14 days from when Ivy Inc. pays the sum of $250."

> An agreement that is silent about what happens where an unwanted act is done may as well be condoning the unwanted act.

Deterrence for Wrong-Doings

People rarely start a relationship with the intention to contravene their obligations. However, contraventions do occur deliberately or otherwise. It therefore helps to have set rules to address the question "what happens where a party contravenes the contract?".

An agreement that is silent about what happens where an unwanted act is done may as well be condoning the unwanted act. It is therefore usually helpful to state the punishments for any act done contrary to what was agreed.

Similarly, any particular remedy that a party envisages it may need should be specifically stated in the contract. This is important because the gravity of wrong doings may vary. Where people that signed an agreement expressly state the consequences of a contravention, there will not be a need to consider the weight to be attached to the wrong in determining the sanction since parties already agreed on the applicable sanction. Having sanctions stated in a contract does not mean that the innocent party's right will be limited to only those sanctions (except the contract expressly states so). The rights provided by general law to protect contracting parties may be explored, in addition, where there is a wrong doing by any of the parties. Some of the rights include: right to seek for damages, specific performance, recission or restitution.

Below is an example of a deterrence clause:

> "If Joe is unable to deliver the cocoa seeds on
> or before 14 days from when Ivy Inc. pays

the sum of $250, Ivy Inc. may terminate the contract and demand for money paid and a default sum of $50 which must be paid within 3 days of demand".

SCENE 11

Joe's bedroom at night...

Joe goes through the files in the brown envelope labeled "Ivy Inc." while attempting several futile calls. Seated in front of the mirror is Eve trying to take off her make-up.

Eve: (breaking the long silence) Baby, what's going on? You've been silent and putting on an alligator face since I got back.

Joe: It's my client abroad; the cocoa contract. They are yet to receive the container of the seeds and the deadline is fast approaching.

Eve: And what's the deterrence in the deal?

Joe: If I fail to deliver the cocoa seeds 14days after Ivy Inc. pays the full sum of $250 as agreed in the contract, they may terminate the contract and demand a refund and default sum of $50 which must *be paid within 3 days of demand.*

Eve: Oh my God Joe! You didn't mention this. What are we going to do now?

Joe: I'm sorry. I'm so confused right now. I really do not know what to do. My head is spinning like…

Eve: Calm down (patting his face), try to rest, everything will be alright. By tomorrow we will contact our lawyer and tell her about the situation so we know what to do about it. It's okay sweetheart, alright? Let us have our meal.

FADES

Conflict Management Measures

Conflict in itself is not bad when it is viewed from the fact that we are social beings with feelings and a sense of right and wrong. The best of relationships go sour sometimes and the way to give hope to the relationship is by agreeing on conflict management measures. There is a bias against court adjudication in cases of contract relationship; it is often said that "you do not go to court to make friends". The court system is known to be time consuming and cumbersome too.

Most times, the fate of transactions is handed to lawyers who may sometimes have no empathy towards the relationship between their clients. Similarly, confidential transactions are exposed to public scrutiny by reason of the decision to go to court. For those reasons, people prefer to submit their contract relationship to dispute mechanisms unconnected with the court. Examples include direct negotiation, mediation, arbitration, conciliation, etc. Below is a sample of a conflict management provision:

> "Ivy Inc. and Joe agree to submit any dispute arising under this Agreement to binding arbitration in New York, United States of America".

Conclusion:

The highlighted points are some of the most generic clauses that you will find in contracts. Nevertheless, the peculiarity of each transaction may determine the additional points to be included.

CONTRACT DEFAULTS AND HOW TO HANDLE THEM

The basis of a contract is that there is an agreement to do or otherwise refrain from doing something, else failure will be met with some form of punishment. While this represents the conventional basis of an agreement and emphasis is placed on penalty for default, the modern deal maker must move from that tradition to negotiating for more rewards for excellence.

A client engaged our Firm, sometime ago, to assist with putting together a legal framework for an ingenious idea. Ideally, it was going to take us over six months to structure the idea but the client wanted it achieved within four weeks! We took the safer option of six months and struck a deal for an incentive if we were able to get the job done within four weeks.

There are times when, contrary to the contract, someone fails to perform obligations without any excuse. There could also be a partial performance of obligation which did not meet the extent of performance that was agreed upon. We will look at these situations (in addition to others) and then see how these situations can be dealt with.

Just before we start the journey, let us do a refresher:

Contract is built on the voluntary understanding between people such that there is freedom to agree on anything concerning the contract if those things are not illegal.

More so, a contract is first usually interpreted based on what was agreed upon before the application of legal principles to uncover situations.

SCENE 12

Eden Garden...

The open space is luxuriously decorated with embellishments of gold and black- furniture with soft music playing. The guests chat as they walk around the exhibition. The atmosphere is festive except for Eve whose make up couldn't hide the worry and anger on her face. She hurriedly walks from the garden towards the gate where a bus with the inscription "ABC Foods" hurriedly parks. As she approaches the corpulent woman who was in a near kneeling position, Eve begins to rant.

Eve: Madame I have told you! I shouldn't be begging about this; we had an agreement for 12noon and you are coming to deliver at past 2pm for me? To do what? Guests are beginning to leave. You know what? Don't bother. We have gotten an alternative. Just do us a refund.

Madame Bee: (stuttering) Ca... Can we... (Struggling to speak and pointing helplessly towards the Garden as if to inquire if they could start serving the almost empty hall). Madam, and we no mean am o! The thing just happen like that and before we close eyes open, time don run finish

(Trying to explain that she did not deliberately delay).

Eve: I will have none of those excuses. You signed an agreement, didn't you?

Madame Bee: Madam, I no mean am like that o! Na why I be dey beg you... (explaining that the delay was not intentional and at the same time apologising)

> *Eve: Nobody signs an agreement on which they intend to default!*
>
> **PAUSE**

If ABC Foods' Agreement with D-Logistics reads:

"Failure to deliver the meal at the agreed time will be treated as a serious breach which permits D-Logistics to excuse itself from the Contract, claim the total sum paid and an additional $10 as compensation for the default"

That means that Eve's company may decide to let go of the contract, demand for a refund of the money paid and also ask for $10 as compensation for ABC Foods' default.

If ABC Foods assured that its meals are served in plastic plates but ends up delivering its food in foil plates, D-Logistics may not necessarily renege from the contract but can claim compensation for breach of warranty. Compensation in this situation can be calculated by analysing the value of what should have been used for the supply as against what was used for it. The cost difference then becomes the extent of compensation that may be claimed. Where the

Agreement expressly mentions that the use of plastic plates is fundamental or where the importance of using plastic plates can be reasonably deduced from the reading of the entire agreement, Eve's company may be able to make a claim for breach of condition.

Assuming there was no agreement, D-Logistics may have to fall back on standard practices and rely on "the test of a bystander" (also known as "a reasonable person's test") by which rights and responsibilities are resolved through the question "what will be the decision of a reasonable person in the circumstances?" There would then be a need to do an analysis of the value of the loss caused by ABC Foods as a result of its default.

Eve's company can save itself all the stress, if it simply ensures that there is a written agreement which states roles and consequences for any default.

Types of Default

You may list instances that will amount to default and the consequences of each of the instances. This will help your business in many ways including:

■ It helps everyone know the obligations that are of the utmost importance in the relationship.

■ It aids speedy conflict resolution since everyone has agreed on what amounts to a default and consequences for those defaults.

If you do not highlight instances and their consequences or a default happened which was not envisaged or sufficiently captured in the Agreement, then, there may be a need to bring in the "reasonable person's test" as earlier mentioned.

"The reasonable person's test" is not a magic wand. To that extent, there are principles that are well established and used to decide whether a default is minor such that you may be entitled to compensation but not a release from the Agreement, or major, such that you can immediately put an end to the contract and also claim compensation. Below are key things that you should know:

■ The key word for a major breach is that a party either failed to meet obligations under the agreement or did something substantially different from what everyone agreed would be done. In essence, if ABC Foods was engaged to deliver packs of snacks but went on to deliver cocktail drinks, a by-stander has the role of answering if ABC Food's performance is substantially different from what was agreed and if that is so, then, Eve may put an end to the contract and claim compensation.

■ If there was performance of what everyone agreed but the performance did not meet the expectation, it might be considered as a minor breach. In essence, if ABC Foods delivered packs of snacks as agreed but the delivery was done a little late from agreed time, it may be considered as a minor breach which will not excuse Eve from performing her own obligations under the contract, even though she may claim compensation for the delay.

■ If from the nature of a person's obligations, it is reasonable for "time" to be of importance, then the inability of that person to meet the obligation may be considered as a major breach. In essence, if ABC Foods delivered meals after the exhibition had ended, it may be viewed as a major breach and the consequence will be that Eve may put an end to the contract and claim compensation.

POSSIBLE EXCUSES BY A DEFAULTER

Sometimes, a deal may go wrong unintentionally. In the same vein, it is not in all situations that default may have been intended. A person may therefore be in default and have a limited liability or even be excused from any liability. Let us look at some of these situations:

1. **Invalid or Illegal Contract:** A contract that is tainted with invalidity or illegality cannot be enforced. It is usually said that you cannot build something on nothing. For instance, if Charles agree to clear a box of illegal substance, he may not validly make any claim on the contract where there is a breach.

At the time of tidying up this book, many countries imposed laws restricting movement and public activities due to a global pandemic. If Eve mandates ABC Foods to supply meals in disregard of government order for lockdown, ABC Foods cannot be sued for refusal to supply the meals during the lockdown period and the company cannot likewise claim any benefit from the contract.

2. **Inability to perform an obligation due to an event which is beyond a person's control and due to nobody's fault** (i.e.

Frustration of Contract). Where this happens, the parties may be excused from being liable for default. The doctrine of frustration of contract is essential to businesses and is therefore discussed in detail in the next chapter.

YOUR RIGHTS AGAINST A PERSON IN DEFAULT

Where an agreement is being treated with disdain by a party to the agreement, the other party might have some rights. Those rights will to a large extent be dependent on the agreement signed by both parties and the exact disdainful action and its effect.

Generally speaking, the rights will include:

1. Right to terminate the agreement: Depending on the nature of default, you may be entitled to a right to discontinue the agreement. If you desire to exercise this right, it is advisable that you communicate expressly to the defaulting party to let the party know that you have opted to terminate the agreement. That way, there is no unnecessary presumption that you have condoned the default. Recently, the CEO of an emerging tech company consulted us regarding his engagement with his employer, the company's management decided to slash his pay without first discussing the pay slash with him, so he wanted to know what his rights were (if any).

One of the things we encouraged him to do was to communicate his disagreement about the reduction to the management, especially bearing in mind that it was a decision made without his consent.

If you fail to communicate within a reasonable time of default, you may be presumed to have waived (condoned) the default. Whichever way, you should always ensure that your written agreement clearly states that a refusal to enforce rights where there is a default does not amount to condonation of the default.

2. **Right to compensation: You** may have this right especially if you have been made to suffer some form of loss as a result of the other party's default. Your right to compensation may include general compensation and compensation for specific loss incurred as a result of the default.

3. **Right to a refund:** Where some payment was made, you may be able to request refund of the sum paid.

4. **Right to apply to a court to compel the defaulting party to compulsorily perform contract obligations.** Although this right may not apply if compensation can be sufficient to appease for the default.

PLAY

SCENE 12 (continues)

Madame Bee: E get as tins be for this locking period (referring to the lockdown period).

To travel go buy food materials get k-leg.

If to say I know say na so this convid period go be, I for no gree do this work

Na beg I dey beg Iya Oko mi (my husband's mum), ndo (please)!

Eve: You this woman ehn! You and your comedy... Ok, tell your boys to set up fast and serve the guests now. We deserve that you compensate us for your lateness.

Madame Bee: That one no be problem at all. Thank you (almost bending to her kneels). Oya Godwin! Make una go begin set up serve the guest. (Shouting) Where Maleek?! You don start again abi?

FADES

FRUSTRATION OF CONTRACT

There are instances in peoples' lives when certain things do not go as expected due to nobody's fault. Nature sometimes takes the blame and we refer to those situations as "acts of God". The effect of that kind of situation is that it either halts responsibilities (if the event is of a temporary consequence). Otherwise, it aborts the contract as a whole if obligations can no longer be performed. Let's look at some instances and a scene to learn more.

Instance 1:

Ivy Inc. a company registered under the laws of Texas engaged Joe to source for and supply cocoa seeds from Africa, he was to get the task done within 14 days. Unfortunately, a virus pandemic occurred thereafter by reason of which movement was restricted across all countries to avoid the spread of the virus. What happens to the contract between Joe and Ivy Inc.?

SCENE 13

An eatery...

Joe with a pack of food is trying to make his way towards the exit when he bumps into his friend, Texas.

Texas: Joe! Joe!

Joe: Sup Pal! How're you doing? (Both exchange elbow shakes)

Texas: I'm good. How are you doing? How is Eve too?

Joe: She is well and bubbling as ever. What are you doing here?

Texas: I run supplies for them here so I came to make some enquiries. Meanwhile, how far with that deal with Ivy Inc.? Have you been able to supply them?

Joe: Mehn! I haven't supplied. The Covid-19 pandemic broke out a few days to the delivery deadline and many countries closed borders to avoid the spread of the virus.

PAUSE

Analysis:

The principle of "frustration of contract" is used to refer to an event which makes completing contractual obligations impossible. When that happens, the contract may be said to have been frustrated.

The first question to ask is whether the event is such that makes the performance of the obligation impossible or inconvenient. If it makes it impossible, then the contract may be said to be frustrated. However, if it merely makes it inconvenient, it may mean that the contract is not frustrated.

Looking at the deal between Ivy Inc. and Joe, performance may not be possible if he cannot arrange for the transportation of the cocoa seeds, so, we may conclude that he is being frustrated from carrying out his obligation.

Did you notice too that there is a time limit for him to deal?

What the time factor does is that it determines whether frustration is permanent or temporary. If the lockdown is such that it would last longer than the three weeks period, it means that the contract itself has been frustrated. In that case, Ivy Inc. and Joe may have to let go of the contract or agree on a new arrangement.

PLAY

Texas: So, what are you going to do now?

Joe: I intend to discuss the situation with my lawyer. We might make a request to the company for a new arrangement or something

Texas: I trust you will handle it well. Let me release you before you are late.

Joe: Alright. Thanks big man. We will see later.

FADES

What if the movement restriction started after the three weeks period meant for Joe to supply the cocoa seeds? Can Joe be excused by reason of the movement restriction? The answer is NO, because Joe was already in default before the restriction. In essence, where someone has failed to carry out an obligation within the agreed time, the person cannot excuse non-performance by claiming that an event beyond their control later occurred.

Furthermore, the frustrating event must not be a remote reason but the main reason for non-performance.

Finally, what if Joe had already supplied some cocoa seeds before the restriction of movement?

Frustration affects agreement from the point of the frustrating event. So, the supply earlier made by Joe remains valid. In apportioning benefits and responsibilities, there may be a need to be guided by the Agreement between Joe and the company (if any). Where that is non-existing or where the situation is not captured in the Agreement, Joe may be able to recover expenses and entitlements up until the period of the frustrating event.

Let us revisit two instances that we shared earlier

Instance 1:

Dave, a lawyer offers to prepare AN AGREEMENT in his private capacity but dies and the client finds out about his demise after accepting to give the job to him.

Analysis:

Dave's death, no doubt, means he cannot be expected to carry out the task again. Besides, the contract is such that it is personal to him. In essence, he was the one engaged (not his law office) and he is the one to do the task too. His death therefore means that the deal is frustrated as far as it has to do with him and the client. If money has been paid to Dave, the Executors/Administrators of his Estate may be made to repay especially since his task under the deal is yet to be performed.

Instance 2

Ivy Inc. makes an offer to Joe Investments Limited (SJIL) and SJIL communicates that it accepts the offer without knowing that Tom (CEO of Ivy Inc.) died shortly after the offer was communicated.

Analysis:

The first thing you might have noticed here is that Tom acted on behalf of his company. Secondly, an incorporated company is usually known as an "artificial person" because it can sue and be sued in its name, own property in its name and do almost anything that humans can; it can give birth (Group of Company/Holding Company), it can have children with distinct names and personalities (subsidiaries), it can be rich while the founder is broke and it can continue to exist even after the death of its founder. Upon registration, it becomes distinct from its founders, the same way a child is separated upon birth by cutting the umbilical cord.

In essence, Tom is different from Ivy Inc. and his death will not "frustrate" an offer which he signed on behalf of the company.

SCENE 14

Joe and Eve are preparing for their wedding anniversary. They contracted the services of ABC Foods to prepare 50 plates of food but the anniversary did not eventually hold. Now, they want a refund from ABC Foods and have engaged their lawyer to sue ABC Foods...

PAUSE

What do you think?

Analysis:

It is not sufficient that an act has made performance impossible, that act must also be such that affects something that forms the mutual basis of the Agreement. If ABC Foods Company agreed to supply 50 plates of food without knowing that Joe and Eve's purpose of engaging it was because of their wedding anniversary, the couple may not be able to rely on the doctrine of frustration of contract to make a claim for refund.

What if ABC Foods knew about the upcoming wedding anniversary and also knew that the contract to supply food was because of the wedding anniversary? Can ABC Foods insist on not refunding money paid once Joe and Eve have cancelled the event?

Analysis:

As earlier stated, an agreement is usually first interpreted based on what parties expressly agreed before the application of legal principles and doctrines to uncovered situations. In essence, If Joe and Eve signed to a "no-refund" agreement, they may not be able to claim a refund even in the face of the fact that unforeseen events happened and they could not go on with their planned wedding anniversary.

Further Question:

If the Agreement with ABC Foods does not have a "no-refund" policy and ABC Foods was yet to commence its tasks, can the company be excused from refunding money?

Analysis:

The principle of frustration of contract relieves parties from further obligations not the consideration.

In essence, while ABC Foods may be excused from supplying the plates of food, it does not excuse it from refunding the money paid for the task.

LETTING GO AND MOVING ON FROM RELATIONSHIPS

Every relationship has a way of coming to an end, even the profound ones! The maxim of the law is that "a document speaks for itself". So, if you have a written agreement with another, it may be important to look at the agreement to see if it states anything about how to move on from the contract.

Most employment contracts would usually provide that parties give notice of intention to move on from the contract or pay instead of notice.

If a contract has a portion that talks about how to terminate the contract, until that portion is followed or there is a breach, the contract may continue to exist.

A contract may end as a result of a number of things. It may be a happy ending for all in which case it might be said that the parties have "performed" and the agreement has come to an end.

Parties may also "agree" to move on from the relationship. It could be that one or more of the parties have contradicted the contract itself and the innocent party opted to move on from the relationship as a result of "breach".

It might just be a case of inability to perform a contract as a result of a supervening event that is beyond control in which case everyone might decide to close the deal and move on. It is safer to always communicate any of such inabilities to the other party promptly.

Agreement: Parties may simply decide not to carry on again with a contract. Sometimes too, parties may renegotiate and end up substituting one contract with another. This is sometimes referred to as "novation of contract". A client once asked our Firm to substitute the retainer for one of their subsidiaries which was to be liquidated to another subsidiary such that the contract to give legal support to the defunct subsidiary is brought to an end and all rights, privileges and obligations subsequently goes to the existing subsidiary just like a new contract.

Other times, it could happen that parties agreed to adjust one or more areas of their agreement. This is usually known as "variation". Whether it is moving on, novation, variation, etc., the effect of all of these is to bring the initial agreement to an end.

Frustration: This has been discussed earlier. A typical example of a frustrating event is death. If the contract is a contract that binds a single individual as different from a group or company and a party becomes incapacitated or dies, the contract may be said to have come to an end. "Marriage" is a popular example of personal contract. A popular recitation of marriage the contract goes:

> "To have and to hold from this day forward,
> for better for worse, for richer, for poorer, in
> sickness and in health, until death do us part"

It is for that reason that those who bind themselves to the marital vows owe each other a duty to continue the union until death, except there is a supervening event that led to a divorce.

Another example of a frustrating event is government laws and regulations. Many artists were billed to perform at events prior to the Covid-19 pandemic that broke out in the year 2020 but they could not perform due to government regulations for lockdown, social distancing, etc. Around that period too, there were government regulations to limit gatherings to a certain number of people. In essence, it became illegal for some kind of congregations to converge.

Sometimes, you can negotiate termination if you are the one seeking to move on. It is safer to have your termination negotiation in writing such that you are not considered in breach.

SCENE 15

Joe's office...

Genie, Joe's lawyer, after listening to Joe's plight, tries to suggest possible solutions.

Genie: With what you have said, there's only a little that can be done at this stage. You should have communicated your inabilities promptly to Ivy Inc.

Joe: Like letting them know there was no way I could have met the deadline as a result of the pandemic?

Genie: Yes, that the contract was frustrated. Nevertheless, I will deliberate on the situation and see what I can do about it while you still try to get in touch with the exporters. Let us try to renegotiate the contract especially considering that the Covid-19 pandemic is a global outbreak.

Joe: Alright! Just do what you can for me please. Thank you so much. Have a nice day.

FADES

SCENE 16

Anderson Law Practice, Genie's Law Office mails Ivy Inc. requesting for contract variation with Joe. The basis of the request is highlighted in precise words while Ivy Inc. is urged to respond within 7 days of receiving the email.

SCENE 17

It's been one week now and no response yet from Ivy Inc.

Genie and Joe are seen plotting their next move.

Joe: Hey Genie, how about we get you in a lamp to work some magic on this contract for me?

Genie: Ha-ha! Except that you are not Aladdin!

(laughter)

As they continue to mumble, Joe's phone beeps. It is an email from Tom, the CEO of Ivy Inc. rejecting Joe's offer by altering it to place a new offer suitable for both parties. Joe quickly shows the mail to Genie for her view since his substituted offer is automatically terminated. Genie deliberates on it with keen attention.

Joe: (after some minutes) What do you think? I think it's a good offer after all?

Genie: (assertively) Yes, it is. It is a favourable one. You may choose to accept it.

Joe: Alright. (shifting his gaze to the MacBook on his desk) Let me communicate my acceptance now. No time to waste. Sent. All done! Thank you Genie, we should drink to this.

Genie: Nice! Less alcohol though

(Joe's secretary comes in)

Secretary: I'm sorry to interrupt sir but you need to see this.

Joe: (Takes the mobile device from him) What's that? ...Tom! Dead? Cardiac arrest? How? (hands the device over to Genie) ...What's going to happen now?

Genie: We are safe. Since Ivy. Inc. made an offer to you and you have communicated your acceptance of the offer without knowing about Tom's demise shortly after the offer was communicated. More importantly, Ivy Inc. is an artificial person in the eyes of the law and has a legal personality distinct from Tom, its CEO.

Joe: (Very excited) Really!!! You just saved and made my day. We should drink to this.

Genie: Drink to what again exactly? To celebrate your deal or mourn the dead?

Joe: Erhh...That was kind of insensitive though. Anyway, life goes on.

FADES

WRITE IT

A final thought!

As a business owner, entrepreneur or leader, you are more secure if you ensure that your discussions are written and that parties eventually sign an agreement. A friend once mentioned that it is important to put everything in black and white when everyone is still smiling.

Having your discussions in black and white may not be realistic at all times. Nevertheless, you can make it a point of duty to recap conversations through email, text message, etc.

"Write it" does not mean that you must always prepare agreements for all conversations. Rather, it is a call for you to have a systematic process of reducing discussions to written form. You will earn your client's respect and win more deals when you are that detailed in your affairs.

As lawyers, we find that it is easier to prove a contract when it is documented. It is also easy to prove the terms of contract especially the dos and don'ts when everything is spelt out. Does it mean that an oral agreement is not enforceable? No, that is not the intention. The emphasis is that it is easier to prove a written contract.

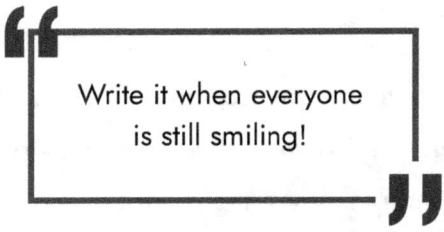

For oral agreement, the basis of proof may have to be predicated on whether there was third party evidence, some recordings or other indirect proof. That is, whether someone else was there and aware of what parties agreed, what was said and what was promised because it is your word against the person's. So, if you say "A" and the person says "no, it was "B"", you have a duty to prove that parties agreed on "A". The obligation to prove what was agreed and what was not agreed has cost many businesses a fortune. That should not be you, so WRITE IT!

www.ingramcontent.com/pod-product-compliance
Lightning Source LLC
Chambersburg PA
CBHW060851220526
45466CB00003B/1322